The Ultimate Questions Book ~ Life Purpose

Copyright © 2013 Marketing Tao, LLC. All rights reserved. No part of this material shall be used for any purpose other than intended. Nor shall any part of this product or the materials included be reproduced by any means, including electronically stored, without the written permission of Kathy Jo Slusher and Marketing Tao, LLC.

The Ultimate Questions Book ~ Life Purpose

Table of Contents

Skillful Questioner 2

Powerful Questions 6

How to Use 9

Additional Use 11

Open/Closed-Ended Questions Chart 14

General Life Purpose Questions 15

Life Purpose Wheel 45

Passion Questions 46

Mission Questions 48

Vision / Dream Questions 50

Inspiration Questions 52

Skills & Talents Questions 54

Values Questions 56

Legacy Questions 58

Ideal Role Questions 60

Life Purpose Values / Quality Assessment 62

Blank Wheel 64

Life Purpose Quotes 65

SMART Goals Checklist 74

About the Work 75

About the Authors 76

Additional Resources 77

The Skillful Questioner

Problems cannot be solved by the same level of thinking that created them.
    ~ Albert Einstein

During the Renaissance there was a massive resurgence of learning and a gradual yet widespread shift in education, leading to economic growth and development, political and social reform, and an increase in trade and commerce.

The Industrial Revolution was a major turning point in human history. There were immense technological advancements, economic progress, income & population growth, and an increase in the standard of living never seen before.

Why?

They were asking themselves powerful questions that shifted the way they approached problems, and spurred curiosity and creativity.

Today, we are on the verge of another major shift. To make the leap we need to make we must ask ourselves and our clients questions that achieve & surpass that same level of curiosity and creativity.

The quality of questions we ask directly influence the knowledge we acquire and the actions we take.

By asking quality, empowering questions we can find the answers leading to the change we seek.

Being a skillful questioner is more than just the words used in the questions. It's as much about how you ask the questions as it is about the words you use. Having no attachment to the outcome of the question and addressing the questioner with curiosity, objectivity and in a non-confrontational manner creates an atmosphere of safety for the questionee to answer honestly and thoroughly.

With over 30 years of coaching, training, facilitation, and experiential learning experience between the two of them, both Denny & Kathy Jo recognize even the most skilled professionals can sometimes get stuck finding the right questions.

Asking powerful questions allow the questionee to see things differently, open up creativity, gain new perspectives, see solutions, discover their own answers, deepens relationships and trust, and improves problem-solving and decision-making abilities.

You can ask the most empowering questions and unlock amazing possibilities, but unless you truly listen and the questionee feels that intent, forward movement is stunted. Listening is an important part of communication as is asking powerful questions. However, not all listening is effective listening.

It is said that hearing is a physical ability. We all hear. We don't always listen. Listening is a skill, one that must be practiced and intentional to be effective.

As a vital part of the questioning process, listening enables:
- The acquisition of new information
- Greater insight to the values, strengths, behavior and needs of the questionee
- The questionee to discover his / her own perspectives of the situation
- Trust & Rapport
- Understanding of underlying meaning
- Motivation
- Depth & Intimacy
- Mutual understanding
- The questionee to feel heard and understood

Levels of Listening

There are 4 Levels of Listening. We have all experienced listening to others and being listened to at each level. The higher the level the more energy is required to maintain that level. Not every conversation you have will take place at the Intuitive Listening level.

1. **Competitive Listening**: The main focus in Competitive Listening is on the listener's own thoughts. Here the listener is more interested in their own views and is waiting for an opportunity to jump in and react.

2. **Attentive Listening**: The main focus in Attentive Listening is on the words being said. There is genuine interest in hearing and understanding what is being said but assumes an understanding, not checking with the questionee for confirmation.

3. **Reflective Listening**: The main focus in Reflective Listening is on a deeper and clarified understanding of what is being said. There is genuine interest in listening, not just hearing, as well as understanding what is being said and confirms that understanding, often through mirroring back the exact information shared.

4. **Intuitive Listening**: The main focus in Intuitive Listening is an understanding of the meaning behind what is said. There is genuine desire to understand not only the meaning of what is being said but also the tone, pitch, speed, of what's being said, the body language that accompanies the words, what is being said behind the words, and what is NOT being said.

We all know how important communication is. However, the vast majority of communication isn't spoken. According to studies done in the '70s by Albert Mehrabian, only 7% of communication takes place through exchange of words. The remaining 93% of information is communicated through body language, eye contact, and pitch, speed, tone and volume of the voice.

Understanding that most information is not communicated through words, to be a powerful listener there are several things you have to keep in mind while listening to the questionee.

Keys to Powerful Listening

1. Intentions are set to gain a greater understanding of the questionee, their behavior, thinking, values, beliefs, perspectives and needs.
2. Stay Curious.
3. Detached Involvement: the ability to tap into deep levels of empathy and place yourself in the questionees position, understanding their thoughts and feelings without taking on their emotions.
4. Focus on what is being communicated in all areas – body language, tone, pace, pitch, energy – while not focusing on your response.
5. Offer feedback and request clarification if necessary.
6. Remember silence is golden. Don't be afraid of silence. Allow the questionee to sit with the question and ponder.
7. Use Intuitive Listening as much as possible.

When entering a conversation where you are required to deeply listen and understand questionees, try your best to enter the situation with as much energy as possible.

Powerful Questions + Intuitive Listening + Acknowledgement + Time to Respond = Unlocked Potential & Possibilities

Making Questions Powerful

Asking the right questions in the right way is key to achieving the right results. Powerful questions immediately access our creative, holistic brain from which solutions are born. These thought provoking questions are designed to forward your client's actions through clarifying, inspiring, probing, challenging, affirming, exploring, opening new possibilities, connecting, assessing, and evaluating, leading to the right solutions for your client.

When crafting questions, there are 3 things you must consider.
1. The Scope of the Question
2. The Construction of the Question
3. Assumptions & Bias in the Question

Scope

The Scope is defined as the range or subject matter that something deals with or to which it is relevant. The scope covers the domain of inquiry. Matching the scope of the question to meet the needs of inquiry increases the capacity to effect change and sets the questionee up for success. Therefore, keep within realistic boundaries of the situation and questionee's knowledge and power.

For example: "How can you best change your perspective?" as opposed to "How can you change the perspective within the organization?"

When determining the scope of your question you must first determine the scope of the answer you are seeking. If you are looking for greater clarification you must ask questions designed to gain clarity. If you are looking for greater insight, you must ask questions designed to go deeper. If you are looking at obstacles you must ask questions designed to uncover blocks. The scope of the answer determines the category of the question to achieve an appropriate response. You can find the question categories under the General Questions section of this book.

Construction

The construction of a question consists of the language, intention and tone you take when asking the question. A question's construction is a critical element in either opening up one's mind to possibilities or closing the mind to solutions. The construction of a question can determine the depth and direction of the answers. Are you looking for a direct yes or no answer? Ask a closed-ended question. Are you looking for deeper clarification? Do you want to open choices or create a new picture? Ask open-ended questions.

The construction of a question stimulates reflective thinking and deepens the conversation. Starting your question with either "who" or "how" determines the level and direction of inquiry. For example: "Who can help you to make this happen?" "How can this happen?"

When constructing the question, ask yourself what "work" you want this question to do.

Assumptions and Bias

Part of being human is that our experiences and perspectives influence the way we think. We all carry with us assumptions and biases. We cannot eliminate them. Awareness of assumptions and biases allow us to be on the look-out for them as we construct and ask our questions, and listen to the answer.

One of the most commonly used questions containing an assumption or bias is "What is wrong?" This question assumes a negative.

Reframing is a potent way to reword questions freeing them of assumptions and bias such as from "What's wrong?" to "What happened?" Reframing encourages deeper reflection and shifts assumptions into possibilities for creating forward action.

A Word About "Why"

Some of the most powerful questions begin with "Why." Some of the most dangerous questions begin with "Why." Why-questions can lead to greater insight and more thorough answers.

They ask the questionee to go deeper and evaluate. Answers to why-questions speak about the inner feelings, beliefs, and motives of the questionee. Because of the highly personal nature of why-questions, safety and trust must be established in the relationship a why-question can easily trigger reactive behaviors and blame detracting from solutions.

The difference between getting greater insight and triggering reaction is the level of safety the questionee feels in the relationship and the way in which the question is asked.

If safety and trust have been established on both sides of the relationship and a why-question is the most appropriate question to ask, stay curious when asking your question. This will keep the non-verbal elements of asking a question as well as your intention on maintaining safety and trust and away from blame.

Choose why-questions carefully and sparingly.

Characteristics of a Powerful Question

1. Solutions-focused
2. Clear & Simple
3. Involves Values & Ideals
4. Generates Curiosity
5. Stimulates Reflection
6. Thought-Provoking
7. Engages Attention
8. Focused
9. Touches Deeper Meaning
10. Leads to More Questions

How to Use This Book

As you encounter a specific challenge around Life Purpose in your or your client's life, you may become stuck and not know where to go next. This book is designed to assist in getting you and your clients unstuck by sparking new, unique, and in-depth questions. You can either use these questions as is or allow them to inspire new ideas for you.

Open / Closed-Ended Questions Chart: Open-Ended questions are designed to require the answerer to go deeper and give more detail. These types of questions should be used as often as possible to gain greater detail, inquiry, and increase understanding. Closed-Ended questions are excellent for commitment. These are used ONLY when looking for a "yes" or "no" response.

General Life Purpose Questions: These general Life Purpose-based questions are a great starting point for coaching around Life Purpose issues. . These questions are designed around basic coaching approach of: clarifying, creating a vision, defining choice, identifying blocks and barriers, evaluating, prioritizing, probing, and scaling. Use these questions as touchstones throughout the process. Categorized based on your client's specific needs and situation, these questions increase the scope of the coaching relationship.

Life Purpose Wheel: The Life Purpose Wheel is a self-awareness assessment you can use for yourself or your client to rate the level of satisfaction in each area related to Life Purpose. You or your client may want to broaden the scope of coaching to encompass each area and clearly define their Life Purpose.

Wheel Specific Questions: As your coaching partnership deepens and gaps in Life Purpose skills present themselves, you can target different areas of Life Purpose more in-depth through these questions. These can even prolong the coaching partnership and develop deeper purpose.

Life Purpose Values / Qualities Assessment: Rating Life Purpose Values / Qualities by how important they are to you and how much you walk your talk can help you identify where gaps may be in your client's Life Purpose Skills. This is an excellent resource in identifying areas and opportunities for growth.

Blank Wheel: Using the Blank Wheel, fill in your or your client's top 8 Life Purpose Values / Qualities and rank these to address the gaps of creating their ideal Purpose in Life. You can also develop new coaching assignments and opportunities around each area.

Life Purpose Quotes: This collection of Life Purpose Quotes is a great resource for either your own marketing efforts or to deepen the level of thinking for your clients. Use these quotes to send inspirational emails, add to your website, use as topics for your newsletters or to Tweet.

SMART Goals Checklist: SMART Goals help ensure success. Goals that are unattainable or unreasonable are a direct line to failure. Failure stifles excitement, passion, and commitment. To ensure the success of your clients, check each goal against the SMART Goals checklist to determine how viable the goal truly is and keep your client's on track.

The Ultimate Questions Book ~ Life Purpose

Additional Uses for This Book

Coaching / Consulting Role

→ Use the Life Purpose Wheel Assessment in a Complementary Session

→ Assess a client's level of satisfaction in the 8 key areas of the Life Purpose Wheel in an introductory session to establish the partnership foundation

→ Use SMART Goals checklist as an evaluation & progression tool

→ Create accountability around the SMART Goals checklist

→ Identify strengths & gaps in each area of the Life Purpose Wheel

→ Identify initial coaching goals

→ Use the questions as preparation for coaching sessions

→ Create customized assignments using the questions

→ Create visualizations & meditations based around the Life Purpose Wheel segments or Questions

→ Use quotes in sessions to stimulate fresh perspectives

→ Add quotes to client emails for inspiration

→ Create a customized assignment by journaling on quotes

→ Create a mastermind or group discussion around a specific quote

→ Help clients set goals using the SMART Goals checklist

Product & Services Development

→ Use this book and the Life Purpose Wheel as your Signature Program

→ Use the Life Purpose Wheel Assessment in a workshop as an assessment or discussion tool

→ Add the Life Purpose Wheel Assessment to your current Signature Program or product

→ Use questions as an idea generator

→ Create an E-course / E-book / E-workbook series around segments of the Life Purpose Wheel

→ Develop workshops & seminars around segments of the Life Purpose Wheel

→ Form Mastermind Groups around key Life Purpose Wheel segments

→ Use Life Purpose Values / Qualities list as an idea generator

→ Write an E-course / E-book / E-workbook on a grouping of Life Purpose Values

→ Create Workshops & Seminars on a grouping of Life Purpose Values

→ Add a quote to a product or presentation for inspiration or point emphasis

→ Use quote in workshop as a discussion topic

→ Use SMART Goals checklist in a workshop as tool to move participants forward

Marketing / Business Development

→ Use the Life Purpose Wheel Assessment as a prospect pre-qualifier

→ Create a prequalifying survey for prospects with questions

→ Use questions or quotes in ezine / newsletter

→ Post a question / quote to your target audience on a LinkedIn Discussion

→ Use a series of questions to outline a promotional teleclass

→ Create a free download of questions around a particular topic

→ Use questions in Blog & Twitter Posts

→ Write an article based on the questions

→ Write an article based on an individual Value

→ Use the Life Purpose Values / Qualities Assessment as a pre-coaching prep form

→ Create an ezine / newsletter around individual Life Purpose Value

→ Post a quote on your blog / Facebook / LinkedIn asking for comments about how it relates to the topic

→ Use a quote to inspire a podcast or video

→ Use quote to motivate article idea

→ Post Quote on Blog / Twitter

Open-Ended vs. Closed-Ended Questions

Open-Ended questions invite others to discuss in detail what is important to them. They are used to gather information, establish rapport, and increase understanding. These questions do not lead and are not geared towards expected outcomes. When used, the asker must be willing to listen and respond appropriately.

Closed-Ended questions are used to elicit a definitive answer. Use only when you want a definite yes or no. They are particularly useful when gaining a commitment.

Ask Open-Ended questions whenever possible.

Open-Ended Questions Start with:	Closed-Ended Questions Start with:
Who	Is
What	Does
How	Are
Why	Do
When	Will
Where	Can

General Life Purpose Questions

Clarifying

Clarifying questions are designed to lay the groundwork and foundation for attaining goals. They set the stage, remove ambiguity, elicit details, and supply known facts.

Ask Clarifying Questions when you need a clear picture of where the questionee is currently at, what resources are available, what perspectives they have, as well as want a picture of where the questionee is coming from, what they want, and the reality of the situation.

Ask these questions as a starting point, to establish a framework.

Example of Clarifying Questions

Questionee: I want to feel more freedom in my life.

Questioner: What do you mean by more freedom?

Questionee: I mean to have the ability to do what I want when I want to.

Questioner: Give me an example.

Clarifying Questions

→ Who knows what your Life Purpose is?

→ Who understands and supports your calling?

→ Who is unsupportive of your calling?

→ Who supports you when things get tough?

→ What does having a Life Purpose mean to you?

→ What is your Life Purpose?

→ What is the worst thing about not having a sense of purpose?

→ What have you learned about your calling so far?

→ What is left to understand?

→ What is your biggest question?

→ Where have you done your best work?

→ Where have your efforts been most appreciated?

→ Where have your efforts been the least appreciated?

→ When have you felt purposeful?

→ When have you felt adrift?

→ When is having a purpose essential?

→ When is having a purpose a liability?

→ Why are you questioning your purpose?

→ Why do you need more clarity?

The Ultimate Questions Book ~ Life Purpose

→ Why is having a purpose in life important to you?

→ Why is it important for you to know about _____?

→ How much energy do you have for this exploration?

→ How do you typically deal with change?

→ How often have you questioned the purpose of life?

→ How often have you felt absolutely sure this is the right path?

Visioning

Visioning questions are designed to establish a desired end result. These questions create a picture of the future so a plan on how to get there can be created.

Visioning Questions allow the questionee to "see" the result they are working to achieve. This opens possibilities, engages creativity, and keeps motivation high and direction clear.

Ask Visioning Questions when creating a new reality, establishing an end-result, identifying the ideal, or giving direction to move forward.

Example of Visioning Questions

Questioner: What would you ideally like to see happen?

Questionee: I would like to move to the country away from the noise and congestion of the city. I would like to grow my own food, and live more simply. I would like to see the stars at night and hear the crickets sing.

Questioner: In this ideal vision, what do you see yourself doing?

Questionee: I see myself writing that book I keep talking about and having time to putter around in my flower garden.

Questioner: How would you feel if you had that?

Questionee: I see myself really happy, living a good life with the people I love, enjoying the things that give my life meaning.

Questioner: That is a beautiful picture for you.

Questionee: Yes it is!

Visioning Questions

→ Who could benefit from your life's calling?

→ With whom can you join to realize your purpose more fully?

→ Who would you like to be?

→ Who would you be if you fully lived your purpose?

→ Who do you want to become?

→ What would you change about your life currently?

→ What would you do if you knew you could not fail?

→ What would your life look like if you loved your work?

→ What would an ideal life look like?

→ What does that ideal vision say about your purpose?

→ If you were in your advanced years and had an opportunity to tell a young adult the most important thing you learned about having a purpose, what you tell them?

→ What would bring out your best?

→ What difference could you make?

→ If money wasn't an issue, what would you do?

→ What would be your dream come true?

→ Where would you like your life's purpose to take you?

→ Where do you want to go?

→ Where would you like to serve?

The Ultimate Questions Book ~ Life Purpose

- → Where in your community could you make a positive impact?
- → Where in the world could you make a positive impact?
- → Where would you like to have an impact?
- → When will you be ready to begin?
- → When will you achieve this dream?
- → When could this happen?
- → When could you see yourself happy and fulfilled?
- → Why would having a clear purpose make a difference?
- → Why do you see things that way?
- → Why is this vision so powerful for you?
- → Why are you imagining that?
- → Why create that?
- → How can you create what you envision?
- → How would you benefit from living a purpose-filled life?
- → How would that creation help you?
- → How would that creation help others?
- → How would you most like to be remembered?

Choice

Choice Questions are meant to show options, empower, and accept responsibility. These questions lend to out-of-the-box thinking and demonstrate options and opportunities.

Ask Choice Questions when questionee feels trapped, hopeless, or feels as though there is no other answer, and needs a new perspective & empowerment to move forward.

Example of Choice Questions

Questionee: I don't know what to do. I really would like to attend that seminar next Saturday and Sunday but my husband wants to take the kids to the cabin that same weekend. We always do everything together.

Questioner: If you knew no-one would be upset, what options do you have to resolve this?

Questionee: You mean, if I went to the seminar and my husband took the boys to the cabin without me?

Questioner: What would happen if that could be the reality?

Questionee: Well that certainly would be different. Maybe that would work. I will talk with my husband tonight.

The Ultimate Questions Book ~ Life Purpose

Choice Questions

→ Who would you be if you stayed where you are?

→ With whom can you align to achieve your dream?

→ Who can you reach out to for support?

→ Who have you avoided?

→ Who has supported your choices in the past?

→ Who has criticized your choices in the past?

→ Who supports that decision?

→ Whose decision is that?

→ What does your purpose require of you?

→ What is yours, and yours alone, to do?

→ What do you really want to do?

→ What difference would you like to make?

→ What is the real decision to make?

→ What are your choices here?

→ What have you avoided making a decision on?

→ What one decision is waiting for you to make?

→ Where would you like to live?

→ Where would you like to work?

→ Where would you like volunteer?

→ Where would you like to travel?

The Ultimate Questions Book ~ Life Purpose

- → Where would that decision take you?
- → Where could that decision take you?
- → When do you need to make that decision?
- → When should this decision be made?
- → When would you like to do that?
- → When do you plan to begin?
- → When has making clear choices been hardest?
- → Why decide now?
- → Why not decide now?
- → Why that particular choice?
- → Why is making a decision crucial?
- → Why would you not take that option?
- → Why are you hesitating with this decision?
- → Why have you decided that?
- → Why would this be your #1 choice?
- → How often do you make clear decisions?
- → How would that choice help you?
- → How might that choice hurt you?
- → How often do you avoid making decisions regarding your dreams?
- → How could this choice help you move forward?
- → How is this choice critical to achieving that goal?
- → How would you like to proceed?

Blocks & Barriers

These questions are designed to uncover & examine what is stopping the questionee from moving forward, seeing progress, and gaining what they truly want.

Ask Blocks and Barrier Questions when you sense hesitation, resistance, goal hopping, or a belief they are unable to move forward.

Example of Blocks & Barriers Questions

Questionee: I really would like to date again but can't seem to put myself out there.

Questioner: What do you think is getting in the way?

Questionee: I'm not sure…..maybe my fear.

Questioner: Fear of what?

Questionee: Fear of not being attractive enough….of no one being interested in me.

Questioner: So you would rather stay home alone where it is safe than risk getting rejected again.

Questionee: As pitiful as that sounds, yes, I think that is it.

Questioner: How well will that work for you?

Questionee: Not very well at all since I want to meet someone! I guess we have some more work to do!

Questioner: I guess we do!

Blocks & Barriers Questions

- → Who might try to stop you from moving forward?
- → Who gets in your way?
- → Who would you become if nothing got in your way?
- → Who disapproves of your chosen path?
- → Who are you trying to please?
- → To whom do you ultimately answer?
- → Who supported your dreams as a child?

- → Who doubts you now?
- → Who taught you to limit yourself?
- → Who in your life has been a dream-dasher?
- → What would you say to them now?
- → What might get in your way?
- → What is holding you back from embracing your purpose?
- → What is your biggest challenge today?
- → What makes that challenge particularly difficult?
- → What false notions about yourself need to go?
- → What are you waiting for?
- → What haven't you considered doing because of fear?
- → What courageous step can you take today?
- → What might try to stop you from moving forward?

The Ultimate Questions Book ~ Life Purpose

- → Where might you be limiting yourself?
- → Where do you set yourself free?
- → Where are you on-purpose?
- → Where are you stuck?
- → Where is your sense of purpose strongest?
- → Where is your sense of purpose the weakest?
- → Where are you blind to your purpose?
- → Where are you deaf to your purpose?
- → Where are you numb to your purpose?
- → Where do you block your creativity?
- → Where do you block joy?
- → Where do you block your sense of adventure?
- → Where in your life does purpose flourish?
- → Where in your life is your purpose stagnant?
- → When does your calling and everyday life align beautifully?
- → When does your calling and everyday life conflict?
- → When have you felt the most purposeless?
- → When are you going to move through that?
- → When have you stopped yourself in the past?
- → When might you stop yourself in the future?

The Ultimate Questions Book ~ Life Purpose

- → When will your purpose and passion align?
- → Why have you struggled with defining your Life Purpose?
- → Why are you uncertain of your life's purpose?
- → Why has this dream gone unfulfilled?
- → Why would that stop you?
- → Why not do it?
- → Why not move beyond that?
- → Why is this particular block so troubling for you?
- → Why is feeling purposeless so debilitating?
- → Why wouldn't you give yourself every chance to succeed?
- → How has your confusion about your purpose affected your relationships?
- → How often to you feel purposeless?
- → How could you continue without knowing your true purpose?
- → How can you get beyond that?
- → If that barrier was a living breathing thing, how would you describe it?
- → How can you get around it?
- → How can you go through it?

Evaluating

Evaluating Questions determine criteria. They evaluate or estimate the nature, quality, extent or significance of situations. They assess factors such as needs, issues, processes, performance, and outcomes. They can also determine the cons of a situation.

Ask Evaluating Questions when the questionee needs to establish a clearer sense of their wants and needs related to a particular situation.

Example of Evaluating Questions

Questionee: I want to achieve more success at work.

Questioner: What would that look like?

Questionee: I would work more efficiently and get things done on time.

Questioner: What would be different if you were more efficient?

Questionee: I would lead meetings with more confidence and get more buy-in from the team.

Questioner: How would it feel if you achieved all of that?

Questionee: Great!

The Ultimate Questions Book ~ Life Purpose

Evaluating Questions

→ Who impacts you the most?

→ Who are you when you are at your best?

→ Who do you believe is living a highly purposeful life?

→ With whom do you feel the most connected?

→ With whom are you the most open about your sense of purpose? Why?

→ With whom are you the least open about your sense of purpose? Why?

→ Who would most benefit from your living on-purpose?

→ Whose sense of purpose most closely aligns with yours?

→ Who offers you the most support?

→ Who attempts to dash your dreams the most?

→ Who believes in your dreams the most?

→ What are the key reasons you are questioning your Life Purpose?

→ What beliefs do you have about your purpose so far?

→ What intrigues you most?

→ What type of people do you gravitate to?

→ What type of organizations interest you?

→ What would suit you best?

The Ultimate Questions Book ~ Life Purpose

- → Where is the best place to go to gain what you seek?
- → Where could you be more on-purpose?
- → Where could you use more support?
- → Where have you been able to live your dream the best?
- → Where have you been able to live wide open?
- → Where has your sense of purpose been the most powerful?
- → Where can you use your skills to make the biggest difference?
- → When are you most engaged with life?
- → When are you the least engaged in life?
- → When would having a career be irrelevant to ones calling?
- → When would it be critical?
- → When would be the best time to pursue that?
- → When is your sense of purpose overpowering?
- → When is your sense of purpose asleep?
- → Why do people need a purpose in life?
- → Why do you need a sense of purpose?
- → Why do you want to explore this more deeply?
- → Why are you willing to take this up?
- → How do you measure success in life?
- → How will you know you have found your true purpose?
- → How important is meaningful work to you?
- → Without them saying a word, how can to tell someone is satisfied with their life?

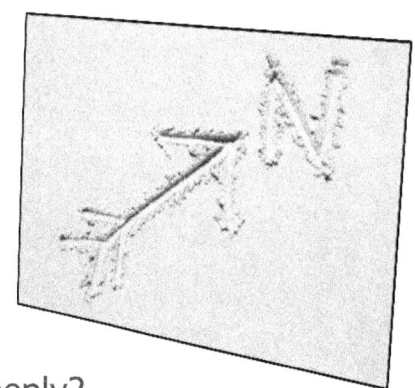

Goal Setting

Goal Setting Questions are designed to move into and forward the action. They include aspects of accountability, step-by-step action, and an understanding of what needs to be done in order to accomplish the desired goal(s).

Goal Setting Questions are intended to set the questionee up for success. In order to accomplish this there are certain factors to be considered when designing a goal plan.

SMART Goals help construct a format for creating successful goals.

Ask Goal Setting Questions when the questionee is ready to move into action.

Example of Goal Setting Questions

Questionee: I decided I want to return to college and finish my degree.

Questioner: That's great! When would you like to begin?

Questionee: Next semester but I have some things I need to do first.

Questioner: What do you see as the 1st step to take to get started?

Questionee: Well, I need to talk with an admissions counselor and figure out what credits will transfer and how many credits I need to complete my degree. Then I have to decide which classes to start with.

Questioner: That sounds like a plan.

When will you make the appointment?

Questionee: This week. I am excited!
    (Move onto creating SMART Goals *pg. 74)

Goal Setting Questions

→ Who can help you implement your plan?

→ Who else supports that?

→ Who might get in the way?

→ Who would you like to include in your plans?

→ Who needs this to happen?

→ What would it take to make the change you seek?

→ What do you need to succeed with that?

→ What is the first thing you need to do?

→ What are the top 3-5 must-haves for your life?

→ What milestones do you need to reach to move you towards your ultimate goal?

→ What do you need in place to start moving forward?

→ When do you want to accomplish that goal?

→ When do you want to begin?

→ When have you set goals before and not followed through?

→ When would you know you have succeeded?

→ When could you achieve this?

→ When are you going to begin?

→ When will you complete this?

→ Where do you imagine this goal will take you?

The Ultimate Questions Book ~ Life Purpose

→ Where could you apply goal setting to achieve your dream?

→ Where in your life will you first notice a difference?

→ Why is reaching that goal important to you?

→ Why is that goal necessary?

→ Why would you stop yourself from achieving that goal?

→ Why not set that goal?

→ Why set that particular goal?

→ How would your life change if those goals were achieved?

→ How would you know you have not succeeded?

→ How would you know you have reached your goal?

Prioritizing

Prioritizing Questions identifies and weighs importance, values and benefits. They can also be used to rank & order.

Prioritizing Questions are great to use in conjunction with Goal Setting Questions and can also help reduce overwhelm.

Ask Prioritizing Questions when the questionee needs to put their priorities in order or examine what is important to them.

Example of Prioritizing Questions

Questionee: I have so many things I need to get done. I feel overwhelmed!

Questioner: That is understandable considering all you have on your plate. Let's make a list of everything you have to do.

Questionee: OK.

(Together they create a list of to-do's)

Questionee: That's a lot! No wonder I feel overwhelmed.

Questioner: I hear you! Let's chunk it down. Of these 12 items, which are the most urgent and necessary to get done this week?

Questionee: I would have to say numbers 3, 6 and 7. The others can wait. I feel much better.

Prioritizing Questions

- → Who do you most want to help?
- → Who would you most like to become part of your inner circle?
- → Who would you become if that was your top priority?
- → Who is your top priority?
- → Who do you need to make more of a priority?
- → Who is the lowest person on your priority list?
- → What would you most like to get out of your life?
- → What would you most like life to give you?
- → What would you most like to give?
- → What are your greatest needs right now?
- → What are your top 3 must-haves going forward?
- → What are the top 3 things your life's purpose wants from you?
- → What changes in the world do you believe need to be addressed first?
- → What is your role in those changes?
- → What message do you keep receiving over and over again?
- → If you could only have one purpose, what would that be?
- → What do you need daily to experience a sense of purpose?
- → What can you do without?
- → What can't you do without?

- → What is your number one priority?
- → Where do you need to set clearer priorities?
- → Where do priorities and purpose cross paths?
- → Where are your current priorities taking you?
- → Where do you want your priorities to take you?
- → When can you make that a priority?
- → When do you need that on the top of your list?
- → When does your sense of purpose influence your priorities?
- → When do your current priorities impact your purpose?
- → Why do you need to make that a priority?
- → Why is that important to you?
- → Why not make that the most important thing in your life?
- → Why are your keeping that on the bottom of your list?
- → In the grand scheme of things, how important is having a purpose really?
- → How certain are you that you need to have a Life Purpose?
- → How willing are you to take that risk?
- → How could shifting your priorities help you stay true to your path?

The Ultimate Questions Book ~ Life Purpose

Probing

Probing Questions make the questionee go deeper, drawing out more details, concerns, challenges, knowledge, and issues about a particular situation. A good Probing Question requires thought. These questions are used to get out the root of the situation, and reveal thoughts, feelings, and details under the surface.

Ask Probing Questions when going deeper into an issue or concern will bring greater insight and help uncover new awareness; thoughts and feelings lying below the surface.

Example of Probing Questions

Questionee: I really don't want to do my presentation tomorrow.

Questioner: Why not?

Questionee: I don't know. Even though I put a lot of time into preparing it, I guess I don't think it's very good. I'd rather hold off until I can make it better.

Questioner: From what you described last time, it appears you have a solid presentation.

Questionee: Yeah, I guess so. I just think it could be better.

Questioner: Putting the presentation itself aside, what are you really worried about?

Questionee: (Pause) That I will freeze…nothing will come out of my mouth and look like a bumbling fool!

Questioner: That is quite a worry.

Questionee: I didn't realize how anxious I am about speaking to the group.

Questioner: How would it be for us to work on that together?

Questionee: Yes, please! That would be great.

Probing Questions

- → Who currently benefits from you living your purpose?
- → Who has the kind of life you admire?
- → Who inspires you to achieve your dreams?
- → Who do you most need support from to make this change?
- → Who in the past broke your dreams?
- → Who in the past supported your dreams?
- → Who has taught you the most about living a life of purpose?
- → Who has most influenced your ideas?
- → With whom did you talk about your dreams when you were a child?
- → With whom do you talk about your dreams?
- → What makes you believe you have a Life Purpose?
- → What have you thought about doing?
- → What is the hardest thing about not knowing?
- → If you had no purpose, what would happen to you?
- → What is the difference between having purpose and living your purpose?
- → What is the difference between a career and a calling?
- → What haven't you tried that would bring you joy?

The Ultimate Questions Book ~ Life Purpose

- → What decision is yours alone to make?
- → What haven't you done that would bring a sense of adventure to your life?
- → What does intuition have to do with discovering your purpose?
- → What would happen if you never did that?
- → What would happen if you lived a purpose-filled life every day?
- → Where does one discover purpose in life?
- → Where can you give your life more meaning?
- → Where have you lived underground?
- → Where have you lived free?
- → Where does life want to take you?
- → Where do you want to take your life?
- → When are you at your very best?
- → When have you felt a keen sense of purpose in the past?

- → When have you felt lost?
- → When might you give yourself every opportunity to realize this dream?
- → When is purpose like a raging sea?
- → When is purpose like a gentle spring rain?
- → Why not do what you have always done? Why risk it?
- → Why has finding your Life Purpose become so critical?
- → How eager are you to discover your true calling?
- → How will you know you are on-purpose?
- → How would someone know you were living the life of your dreams?

New Perspectives

New Perspective Questions are designed to shift the direction of thinking. By shifting thinking the questionee can shift the way they approach the world and situations. These questions often create "aha" moments as they elicit options and possibilities previously not considered.

Ask New Perspective Questions when the questionee persists in levels of thinking that include anger, blame, victim, trapped or when they are unable / unwilling to see alternatives.

Example of New Perspective Questions

Questionee: I think my sister is upset with me.

Questioner: What makes you think that?

Questionee: Because she hasn't returned my calls this week.

Questioner: How certain are you she is upset with you?

Questionee: Well, why else wouldn't she call me back?

Questioner: Great question! What might be some other reasons she hasn't called you back yet?

Questionee: Well, maybe she's really busy with work. I know she had a big project she was working on and her boss can set some tough deadlines. I bet that's it.

New Perspective Questions

→ Who could you talk to about that?

→ Who could give you a fresh perspective?

→ Who are you becoming?

→ Who would you be if everything lined up perfectly?

→ Who can you become?

→ What might be a new way of looking at that?

→ What might be a different way to think about that?

→ What feeling would you like to experience?

→ What new adventure are you aching to have?

→ What would you do if you knew you could not fail?

→ Where is your life's purpose taking you?

→ Where can you find the information you need?

→ Where could your life take you?

→ Where is your heart yearning to break free?

→ Where would you like to give life to your dream?

→ Where would the world be without you?

→ When could you take hold of that?

→ When is your life just perfect?

The Ultimate Questions Book ~ Life Purpose

- → When will you embrace the specialness that is you?
- → When will the world hear your unique voice?
- → Why wouldn't you give yourself every opportunity to be happy?
- → Why is the world devoid without your gift being expressed?
- → Why have you not given birth to that yet?
- → Why does it matter?
- → Why are you waiting?
- → How can you discover what is yours to do?
- → How would others benefit?
- → How would uncovering your true purpose change your life?
- → How would uncovering your true purpose change the life of others?
- → How would you like to help others?
- → How necessary is it for you to share your gifts?
- → How would knowing your life of purpose change you?

The Ultimate Questions Book ~ Life Purpose

Scaling

Scaling Questions help gauge and determine the level of concern, commitment, and importance. They are a tool that identifies where the questionee would position themselves, the situation or determining a level. Scaling Questions can be used to help measure progress, attitude and behavioral change, and situational shifts.

Ask Scaling Questions when the questionee wants to gauge the level of concern, commitment, or importance of a situation or concern.

Example of Scaling Questions

Questioner: On a scale of 1-10, 1 being not at all and 10 being extremely, how important is that for you?

Questionee: I would say about an 8.5.

Questioner: That's pretty important!

Questionee: Yes, it really it.

Scaling Questions

- On a Scale of 1 to 10 (10 = completely satisfied and 1 = completely dissatisfied) where would you rank yourself with your current sense of purpose? Why did you rank yourself that way?

- On a Scale of 1 to 10 (10 = absolutely confident and 1 = not confident at all) how confident are you that you will discover your life's purpose? Why did you rank yourself that way?

- On a Scale of 1 to 10 (10 = absolutely confident and 1 = not confident at all) how confident are you that you will fully live your life's purpose? Why did you rank yourself that way?

- On a Scale of 1 to 10 (10 = absolutely and 1 = not at all) how happy are you with your life as it is? Why did you rank yourself that way?

- On a Scale of 1 to 10 (10 = all the time and 1 = never) how often do you doubt your dream? Why did you rank yourself that way?

- On a Scale of 1 to 10 (10 = completely and 1 = not at all) how fully are you expressing your true gifts? Why did you rank yourself that way?

- On a Scale of 1 to 10 (10 = completely satisfied and 1 = completely dissatisfied) how on-purpose are you? Why did you rank yourself that way?

- On a Scale of 1 to 10 (10 = always and 1 = never) how connected are you with your true purpose? Why did you rank yourself that way?

- On a Scale of 1 to 10 (10 = extremely and 1 = not at all) how optimistic are you about your future? Why did you rank yourself that way?

- On a Scale of 1 to 10 (10 = extremely and 1 = not at all) how passionate are you about your true calling? Why did you rank yourself that way?

Life Purpose Wheel

The Ultimate Questions Book ~ Life Purpose

Directions: for each section of the Life Purpose Wheel, circle the number that represents your current level of satisfaction in that area. The higher the number, the greater your level of satisfaction.

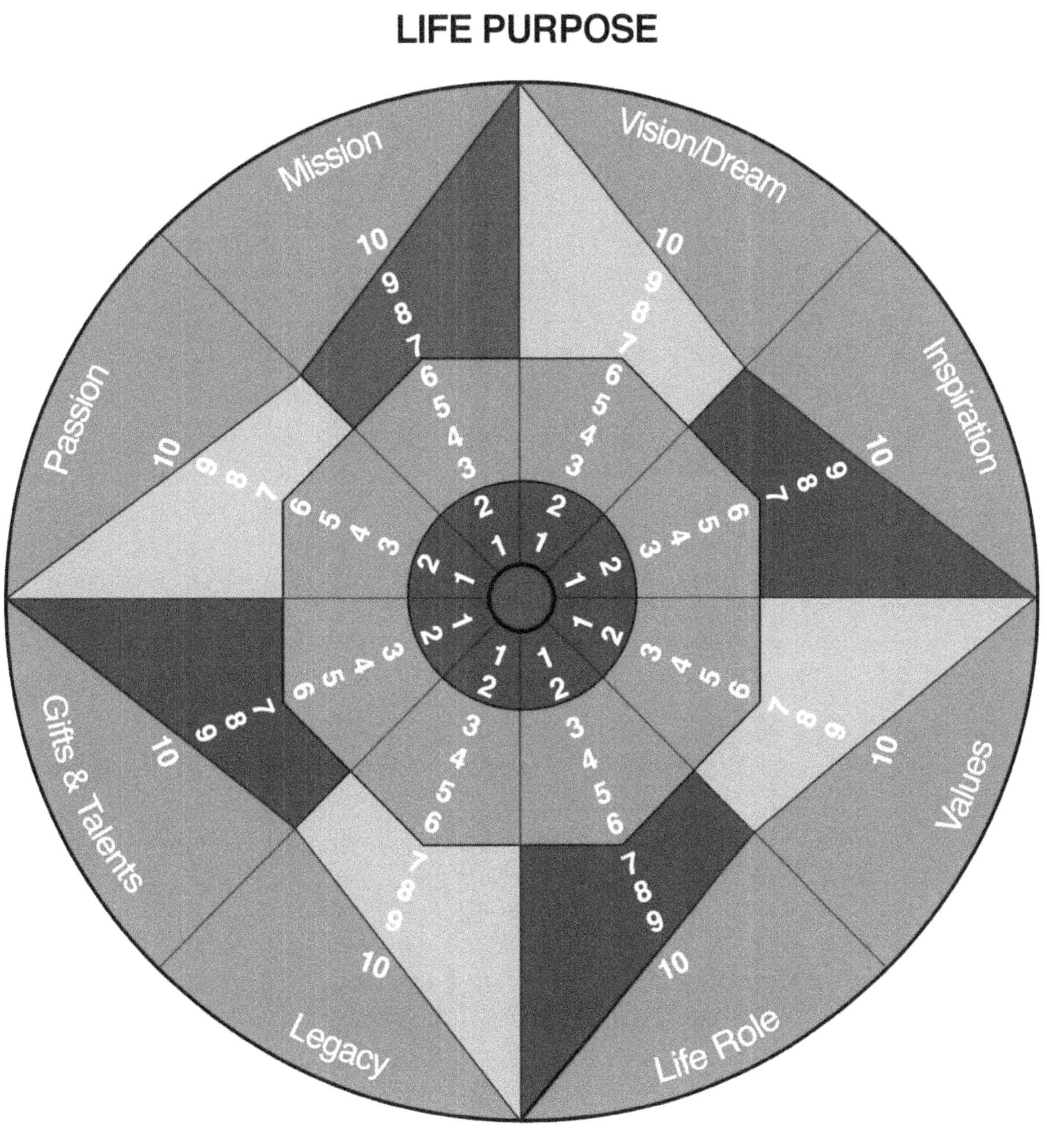

LIFE PURPOSE

© 2013 Unaltered Reproduction Rights Granted, Marketing Tao, LLC

Passion

Who

→ Who would you be without passion?

→ Who exemplifies passion for you?

→ With whom do you have the most difficult time being passionate? Why?

→ With whom do you have the easiest time being passionate? Why?

→ Who would you be if passion fueled your life and / or work?

What

→ What does having passion for your work and / or life mean to you?

→ What are the benefits of being passionate?

→ What is the downside?

→ What three qualities epitomize passion?

→ What could you do to become more passionate in your life?

Where

→ Where does your passion want to take you?

→ Where has passion been missing from your work or life?

→ Where is your passion the weakest?

→ Where is your passion the strongest?

→ Where do you find the passion for this path you have chosen?

The Ultimate Questions Book ~ Life Purpose

When

→ When is passion most essential?

→ When is passion a liability?

→ When would be the best time to engage your passion?

→ When are you the most passionate?

→ When are you the least?

Why

→ Why is passion necessary in life?

→ Why is having passion for what you do important?

→ Why don't you feel passion for that anymore?

→ Why have you lost a sense of passion in your life?

→ Why would you work at something you have no passion for?

How

→ How passionate are you about your current job / career?

→ How passionate would you like to be?

→ How will you begin to reclaim passion for your work?

→ How can passion be cultivated?

→ How would others benefit from your passion?

Your Questions on Passion

→ _____

→ _____

→ _____

→ _____

→ _____

Mission

Who
- → Who inspired your mission into being?
- → Who do you want to help? Why?
- → Who could benefit the most from your mission? Why?
- → Who values your mission?
- → Who needs to understand your mission more fully?

What

- → What is your mission?
- → What do you want your mission to say about you as a person?
- → What inspired you to take up that mission?
- → What supports your mission?
- → What would make your mission stronger?

Where
- → Where do you feel drawn to serve / help others?
- → Where can you make the biggest difference?
- → Where have you made a difference so far?
- → Where does your sense of purpose and your mission intersect?
- → Where does your mission want to take you?

The Ultimate Questions Book ~ Life Purpose

When

- → When are you guided by your mission?
- → When are you disengaged from your mission?
- → When have you seen your mission most strongly expressed?
- → When have you failed your mission?
- → When has your mission failed you?

Why

- → Why is having a mission important for you?
- → Why are those beliefs important parts of your mission?
- → Why would not having a clear mission hinder you?
- → Why are you questioning your true mission?
- → Why do you believe that is your mission?

How

- → How do you express your mission at home, work, in your community?
- → How have you changed the world so far?
- → How would you like to change the world?
- → How could your mission keep you focused?
- → How has your mission been realized in the past?

Your Questions on Mission

- → _____
- → _____
- → _____
- → _____
- → _____

Vision / Dream

Who

→ Who inspires you to dream?

→ Who has dashed your dreams in the past?

→ Who do you need to risk being to see this vision happen?

→ Who do you need support from to make this happen?

→ Who shares your dream?

What

→ What is your vision or dream?

→ What do you need to achieve that?

→ What might stop you from realizing your dream?

→ What three qualities do you need to make this happen?

→ What does your vision have to do with your life's purpose?

Where

→ Where do you envision your life taking you?

→ Where have your dreams taken you in the past?

→ Where do you want to be 10 years from now?

→ Where have you dreamed the biggest?

→ Where have you held yourself back from dreaming about what could be?

The Ultimate Questions Book ~ Life Purpose

When

- → When do you feel the most connected with your vision?
- → When are you the most motivated to achieve your dream?
- → When are you the most disheartened?
- → When have you given up all together?
- → When is it time to reclaim that vision?

Why

- → Why is that a dream of yours?
- → Why does that vision keep coming to you?
- → Why haven't you lived your dreams before now?
- → Why would you let that stop you from realizing your dream?
- → Why is your vision inspirational?

How

- → How could your dream be realized?
- → How does that vision for your life give it more meaning?
- → How would you begin to achieve that dream?
- → How fearless do you need to be to go for it?
- → How would your life be different if you realized your dream?

Your Questions on Vision / Dream

- → _____
- → _____
- → _____
- → _____
- → _____

Inspiration

Who

- → Who inspires you? Why?
- → With whom have you shared your life's purpose?
- → Who lives purpose-driven, inspired lives?
- → Who would you be without inspiration?
- → To whom are you inspired to reach out?

What

- → What does inspiration mean to you?
- → What can you do to cultivate more inspiration?
- → What does inspiration sound like? Feel like? Look like?
- → What would your life look like if you had no inspiration?
- → What is your inspiration guiding you to do right now?

Where

- → Where do you find inspiration?
- → Where is your inspiration the strongest?
- → Where is your inspiration the weakest?
- → Where do you need to rely on your inspiration more?
- → Where could inspiration take you?

The Ultimate Questions Book ~ Life Purpose

When

- → When is your inspiration the strongest?
- → When is your inspiration the weakest?
- → When do you most rely on inspiration?
- → When could inspiration and purpose join as one?
- → When is the best time to listen to your heart?

Why

- → Why is inspiration important?
- → Why are you inspired by that?
- → Why would feeling more inspired be helpful?
- → Why has inspiration eluded you in the past?
- → Why not embrace that inspiration and act?

How

- → How does inspiration guide you?
- → How could inspiration help you determine your Life Purpose?
- → How can you rely on inspiration more?
- → How can you use intuitive guidance to clarify your purpose?
- → How do you inspire & motivate yourself to move forward?

Your Questions on Intuition

- → _____
- → _____
- → _____
- → _____
- → _____

The Ultimate Questions Book ~ Life Purpose

Skills & Talents

Who

→ Who appreciates your talents?

→ With whom do you like to share your skills and abilities?

→ From whom do you hide your talents? Why?

→ Who would benefit the most from your talents?

→ Who would you be if your innate talents came fully alive?

What

→ What is your greatest talent?

→ What skills and talents align with your life's purpose?

→ What doubts about your abilities are living inside you?

→ What talents have you consistently used in your life?

→ What talents have gone underground?

Where

→ Where have your talents been used the most? Least?

→ Where could you share your talents more?

→ Where might you doubt your skills and talents?

→ Where is your talent comfort zone?

→ Where do you see your talent taking you?

The Ultimate Questions Book ~ Life Purpose

When

- → When do you ignore, deny, or hide your talents?
- → When do you shine?
- → When are your talents most fully used?
- → When do you find your talents most engaged? Least engaged?
- → When will the world see your talents expressed in all their glory?

Why

- → Why is knowing and believing in your talents important?
- → Why share your talents?
- → Why aren't you using your talents to their fullest?
- → Why is being talented & skilled important?
- → Why do you like using your talents?

How

- → How do you share your gifts?
- → How can your talents and learned skills contribute to your purpose?
- → How have you suppressed your talents?
- → How would you most like to use your skills and abilities?
- → How would the world benefit?

Your Questions on Skills & Talents

- → _____
- → _____
- → _____
- → _____
- → _____

Values

Who

- → Who honors your values?
- → Who finds what you value questionable?
- → Who would you be without your values?
- → Who would you become if you lived by your values every minute of every day?
- → Who holds the same values as you?

What

- → What are your core values?
- → What do your values say about you & your purpose?
- → What career or avocation would best support your core values?
- → What values have been the hardest for you to express?
- → What values have been the easiest to express?

Where

- → Where in the past have your values been compromised?
- → Where have your values and your Life Purpose intersected in the past?
- → Where would you be without your values?
- → Where could your values be more fully expressed?
- → Where have you been the most aware of your values?

The Ultimate Questions Book ~ Life Purpose

When

- → When have you compromised your own values?
- → When do you most need to stand by your values?
- → When have your values saved you from harm?
- → When are you going to embrace your values completely?
- → When could your values help you most in defining your life's purpose?

Why

- → Why is living life according to your values important?
- → Why have you sacrificed your values in the past?
- → Why doesn't that align with your core values?
- → Why is identifying your core values so important?
- → Why should your Life's Purpose be an expression of what you value?

How

- → How do your core values keep you focused on what's important?
- → How can your core values help you embrace your purpose?
- → How often do you make decisions based on your values?
- → How would you like your life to reflect your values?
- → How can you find a career or avocation that aligns with your values?

Your Questions on Values

- → _____
- → _____
- → _____

Legacy

Who

- → Who do you to want help?
- → Who is your legacy being built around?
- → Who will your legacy say you were?
- → Who has benefited the most from your contributions so far?
- → Who would you be without a clear legacy?

What

- → What legacy would you like to leave behind?
- → What is the one thing you want to be remembered for?
- → What would you like your epitaph to read?
- → What is left to do?
- → What haven't you done that you most want to accomplish before your days are over?

Where

- → Where have your contributions been most notable?
- → Where do you want to contribute more?
- → Where do you experience doubt about your legacy?
- → Where are you feeling the proudest about your accomplishments?
- → Where can you build a richer legacy?

When

→ When do you feel best about your contributions? Why?

→ When have you felt the least acknowledged?

→ When is the best time to build a legacy?

→ When do you want to contribute to that cause?

→ When are your contributions most needed?

Why

→ Why is having a legacy you are proud of important?

→ Why would you want to be remembered for that?

→ Why would others benefit from your legacy?

→ Why do you feel a sense of urgency now?

→ Why is being remembered important?

How

→ How does having a legacy serve you?

→ How does having a legacy serve the world?

→ How can you design your life to build your ideal legacy?

→ How do you want to contribute?

→ How would you like to be remembered?

Your Questions on Legacy

→ _____

→ _____

→ _____

→ _____

→ _____

Ideal Role

Who

→ Who are you?

→ Who do you want to be? Why?

→ Who supports your ideal role? Why?

→ Who is critical of your role? Why?

→ Who could benefit the most if you lived your ideal role to the fullest?

What

→ What is your ideal role?

→ What three qualities best exemplify that role?

→ What has stopped you from fully engaging that role?

→ What beliefs influence your role in life?

→ What is different about you when you feel confident in your role?

Where

→ Where have assumed roles helped you in the past?

→ Where have assumed roles hindered you?

→ Where could this ideal role take you?

→ Where would you most like to engage that role?

→ Where could your ideal role best help others?

The Ultimate Questions Book ~ Life Purpose

When

→ When do you ignore, deny, or hide your ideal role?

→ When do you fight against your ideal role?

→ When will you stop the battle and fully embrace who you were meant to be?

→ When will others know you have fully embodied your ideal role?

→ When is the time to begin?

Why

→ Why did you choose that role?

→ Why are you in that role?

→ Why could another role serve you better?

→ Why would that role support your purpose?

→ Why not take on that role?

How

→ How could that role support your life's purpose?

→ How have past roles contributed to your overall purpose?

→ How could you enliven that role more fully?

→ How many times have you failed to embrace your ideal role?

→ How can you set yourself up for success now?

Your Questions on Ideal Role

→ _____

→ _____

→ _____

→ _____

→ _____

Life Purpose Values / Qualities Assessment

Directions: Identify your top 8 Life Purpose Values / Qualities. How closely do you live these Values / Qualities?

☐ Abundance	☐ Daring
☐ Acceptance	☐ Decisiveness
☐ Achievement	☐ Dedication
☐ Action	☐ Delight
☐ Adaptability	☐ Devotion
☐ Adventure	☐ Discipline
☐ Ambitious	☐ Discovery
☐ Assertiveness	☐ Drive
☐ Authenticity	☐ Eagerness
☐ Awareness	☐ Empathy
☐ Balance	☐ Empowerment
☐ Beauty	☐ Encouragement
☐ Being	☐ Energy
☐ Boldness	☐ Enjoyment
☐ Cause	☐ Enthusiasm
☐ Change	☐ Ethical
☐ Clarity	☐ Excellence
☐ Comfort	☐ Excitement
☐ Commitment	☐ Exhilaration
☐ Community	☐ Experience
☐ Compassion	☐ Family
☐ Competency	☐ Fire
☐ Confidence	☐ Flexibility
☐ Connectedness	☐ Flow
☐ Consciousness	☐ Focus
☐ Conviction	☐ Follow-Through
☐ Courageous	☐ Forward Thinking
☐ Creativity	☐ Free Will
☐ Curiosity	☐ Freedom

© 2013 Unaltered Reproduction Rights Granted, Marketing Tao, LLC

The Ultimate Questions Book ~ Life Purpose

- ☐ Fulfillment
- ☐ Generosity
- ☐ Goal-Oriented
- ☐ Gratitude
- ☐ Grounded
- ☐ Growth
- ☐ Guidance
- ☐ Harmony
- ☐ Health
- ☐ Heart
- ☐ Higher-Powered
- ☐ Honesty
- ☐ Hope
- ☐ Humility
- ☐ Humor
- ☐ Imagination
- ☐ Independence
- ☐ Inspiration
- ☐ Integrity
- ☐ Intention
- ☐ Interconnectedness
- ☐ Interdependent
- ☐ Justice
- ☐ Loyalty
- ☐ Meaning
- ☐ Mindfulness
- ☐ Motivation
- ☐ Mutual Support
- ☐ Nature
- ☐ Openness
- ☐ Opportunity
- ☐ Order
- ☐ Passion
- ☐ Patience

- ☐ Peacefulness
- ☐ Power
- ☐ Presence
- ☐ Productivity
- ☐ Prosperous
- ☐ Purpose
- ☐ Relaxation
- ☐ Reverence
- ☐ Risk
- ☐ Security
- ☐ Self-Awareness
- ☐ Self-Esteem
- ☐ Self-Expression
- ☐ Self-Growth
- ☐ Selflessness
- ☐ Self-Realization
- ☐ Simplicity
- ☐ Sincerity
- ☐ Soul
- ☐ Spirit
- ☐ Spirituality
- ☐ Stewardship
- ☐ Synergy
- ☐ Tolerance
- ☐ Transcendence
- ☐ Trust
- ☐ Truth
- ☐ Unity
- ☐ Universal Power
- ☐ Wholeness
- ☐ Will
- ☐ Wisdom
- ☐ Zeal
- ☐ Zest

The Ultimate Questions Book ~ Life Purpose

Blank Life Purpose Wheel

Directions: In the blank sections of the wheel add your top 8 Life Purpose Values / Qualities from the previous assessment. For each section, circle the number that represents your current level of satisfaction in that area. The higher the number, the greater your level of satisfaction.

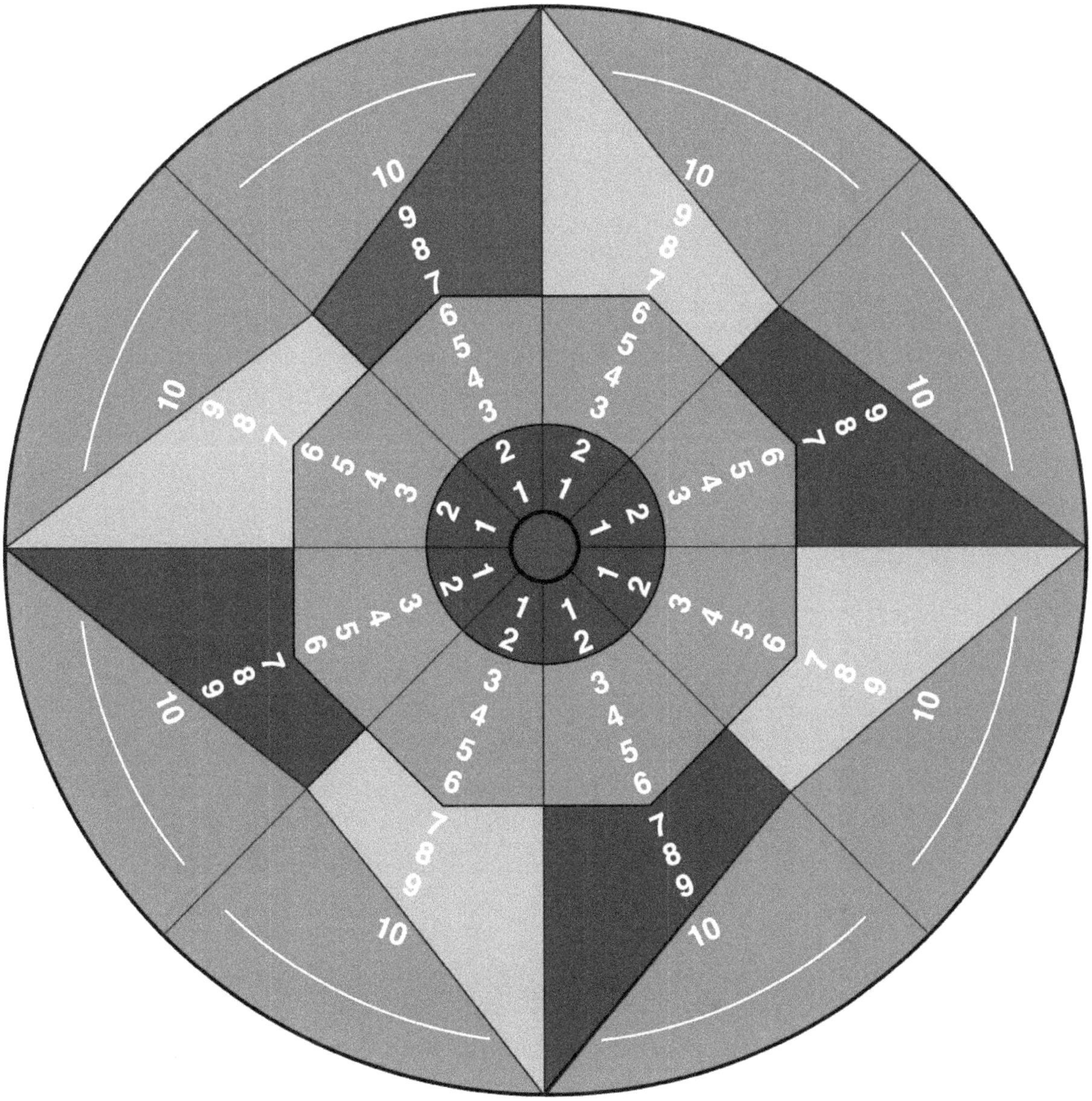

© 2013 Unaltered Reproduction Rights Granted, Marketing Tao, LLC

Marketing Tao, LLC

Life Purpose Quotes

There is only one success—to be able to spend your life in your own way.
 ~ Christopher Morley

The best way to find yourself is to lose yourself in the service of others.
 ~ Mohandas (Mahatma) Gandhi

I am here for a purpose and that purpose is to grow into a mountain, not to shrink to a grain of sand.
 ~ Og Mandino

The secret of success is constancy to purpose.
 ~ Benjamin Disraeli

The purpose of human life is to serve, and to show compassion and the will to help others.
 ~ Albert Schweitzer

The purpose of our lives is to be happy.
 ~ Tenzin Gyatso, the 14th Dalai Lama

Make your work to be in keeping with your purpose.
 ~ Leonardo da Vinci

The purpose of life is a life of purpose.
 ~ Robert Byrne

True happiness... is not attained through self-gratification, but through fidelity to a worthy purpose.
 ~ Helen Keller

Here is a test to find whether your mission in life is finished: if you are alive, it isn't.
~ Richard Bach

Efforts and courage are not enough without purpose and direction.
~ John F. Kennedy

One needs something to believe in, something for which one can have whole-hearted enthusiasm. One needs to feel that one's life has meaning, that one is needed in this world.
~ Hannah Senesh

More men fail through lack of purpose than lack of talent.
~ Billy Sunday

Begin each day as if it were on-purpose.
~ Mary Anne Radmacher

All men should strive to learn before they die, what they are running from, and to, and why.
~ James Thurber

As far as we can discern, the sole purpose of human existence is to kindle a light in the darkness of mere being.
~ Carl Jung

If you're alive, there's a purpose for your life.
~ Rick Warren

Worry ducks when purpose flies overhead.
~ C. Astrid Weber

The way you get meaning into your life is to devote yourself to loving others, devote yourself to your community around you, and devote yourself to creating something that gives you purpose and meaning.
~ Mitch Albom

When you dance, your purpose is not to get to a certain place on the floor. It's to enjoy each step along the way.
~ Wayne Dyer

To me, there is only one form of human depravity — the man without a purpose.
~ Ayn Rand

You will recognize your own path when you come upon it, because you will suddenly have all the energy and imagination you will ever need.
~ Jerry Gillies

To be yourself in a world that is constantly trying to make you something else is the greatest accomplishment.
~ Ralph Waldo Emerson

I think the purpose of life is to be useful, to be responsible, to be honorable, to be compassionate. It is, after all, to matter: to count, to stand for something, to have made some difference that you lived at all.
~ Leo C. Rosten

Hide not your talents. They for use were made. What's a sundial in the shade?
~ Benjamin Franklin

What is a weed? A plant whose virtues have not been discovered.
   ~ Ralph Waldo Emerson

The height of your accomplishments will equal the depth of your convictions.
   ~ William F. Scolavino

Purpose is what gives life a meaning.
   ~ Charles H. Perkhurst

A man who becomes conscious of the responsibility he bears toward a human being who affectionately waits for him, or to an unfinished work, will never be able to throw away his life. He knows the "why" for his existence, and will be able to bear almost any "how."
   ~ Victor Frankl

To have a grievance is to have a purpose in life.
   ~ Alan Coren

Men, like nails, lose their usefulness when they lose direction and begin to bend.
   ~ Walter Savage Landor

Dignity and respect has to do with ... your personal power to make a difference by being true to the best within you and letting that truth shine through your words and actions.
   ~ Gail Pursell Elliott

Man is not born to solve the problems of the universe, but to find out what he has to do... within the limits of his comprehension.
   ~ Goethe

The Ultimate Questions Book ~ Life Purpose

When you are inspired by some great purpose, some extraordinary project, all your thoughts break their bonds: Your mind transcends limitations, your consciousness expands in every direction, and you find yourself in a new, great, and wonderful world. Dormant forces, faculties and talents become alive, and you discover yourself to be a greater person by far than you ever dreamed yourself to be.
~ Patanjali

When we love there is no reason why.
~ Vanna Bonta

It is not our purpose to become each other; it is to recognize each other, to learn to see the other and honor him for what he is.
~ Herman Hesse

The high prize of life, the crowning fortune of man, is to be born with a bias to some pursuit which finds him in employment and happiness.
~ Ralph Waldo Emerson

Too many people overvalue what they are not and undervalue what they are.
~ Malcolm Forbes

What really matters is what you do with what you have.
~ Shirley Lord

I don't want to be a passenger in my own life.
~ Diane Ackerman

You must be the change you wish to see in the world.
~ Mahatma Gandhi

When you see what you're here for, the world begins to mirror your purpose in a magical way. It's almost as if you suddenly find yourself on a stage in a play that was written expressly for you.
~ Betty Sue Flowers

Nothing contributes so much to tranquilizing the mind as a steady purpose — a point on which the soul may fix its intellectual eye.
~ Mary Shelley

Genius is an infinite capacity to take life by the scruff of the neck.
~ Katherine Hepburn

Nothing happens unless first a dream.
~ Carl Sandburg

Twenty years from now you will be more disappointed by the things that you didn't do than by the ones you did do. So throw off the bowlines. Sail away from the safe harbour. Catch the trade winds in your sails. Explore. Dream. Discover.
~ Mark Twain

Every man is the architect of his own fortune.
~ Sallust

Cherish your visions. Cherish your ideals. Cherish the music that stirs in your heart, the beauty that forms in your mind, the loveliness that drapes your purest thoughts, for out of them will grow all delightful conditions, all heavenly environment; of these, if you but remain true to them, your world will at last be built.
~ James Allen

Everybody is talented, original, and has something important to say.
～ Brenda Ueland

To understand the heart and mind of a person, look not at what he has already achieved, but at what he aspires to do.
～ Kahlil Gibran

Strong lives are motivated by dynamic purposes; lesser ones exist on wishes and inclinations.
～ Kenneth Hildebrand

We seek purpose when we are not in touch with who we really are. When an apple tree discovers who it is, the question 'what must I do?' disappears. When you discover who you are (at the deepest place of your being) you will find your purpose.
～ Colleen-Joy Page

I want to sing like the birds sing, not worrying about who hears or what they think.
～ Rumi

We must have a theme, a goal, a purpose in our lives. If you don't know where you're aiming, you don't have a goal. My goal is to live my life in such a way that when I die, someone can say, she cared.
～ Mary Kay Ash

The purpose of art is washing the dust of daily life off our souls.
～ Pablo Picasso

It's never too late to be what you might have been.
～ George Elliot

My passions were all gathered together like fingers that made a fist. Drive is considered aggression today; I knew it then as purpose.
~ Bette Davis

The sum of the whole is this: walk and be happy; walk and be healthy. The best way to lengthen out our days is to walk steadily and with a purpose.
~ Charles Dickens

It is not how much we do, but how much love we put in the doing. It is not how much we give, but how much love we put in the giving.
~ Mother Teresa

There is one quality which one must possess to win, and that is definiteness of purpose, the knowledge of what one wants, and a burning desire to possess it.
~ Napoleon Hill

There is vitality, a life force, an energy that is translated through you; and because there is only one of you in all of time, this expression is unique.
~ Martha Graham

Success demands singleness of purpose.
~ Vince Lombardi

Our prime purpose in this life is to help others. And if you can't help them, at least don't hurt them.
~ Dalai Lama

Try to become not a man of success, but rather a man of value.
~ Albert Einstein

Life has meaning only if you do what is meaningful to you.
~ Alan Cohen

When I chased after money, I never had enough. When I got my life on-purpose and focused on giving of myself and everything that arrived into my life, then I was prosperous.
~ Wayne Dyer

The purpose of life is not to fight against evil and misfortune; it is to unveil magnificence.
~ Alan Cohen

Too many of us are not living our dreams because we are living our fears.
~ Les Brown

S.M.A.R.T. Goals Checklist

Specific
- [ ] What precisely is expected?
- [ ] Be as specific as possible.
- [ ] What will you have when the specific task is complete?
- [ ] What will the outcome be?

Measurable
- [ ] How would you know you have achieved success?
- [ ] How many tasks do you need to do?
- [ ] For how long?
- [ ] Make it a tangible process.

Achievable
- [ ] Is this achievable?
- [ ] What would be achievable?
- [ ] Do you have the skills or resources necessary to meet this goal?

Reasonable
- [ ] Is this a reasonable goal?
- [ ] What might be the obstacles?
- [ ] Considering everything else you have going on, can you achieve this goal?

Time-Oriented
- [ ] When will you be done?
- [ ] When will your tasks be scheduled?
- [ ] How long will it take to accomplish each task?
- [ ] When is the ideal time for this goal to be completed?

About the Work

We live in a time of great change. Faced with some of the most difficult challenges our world has ever known, we feel an urgency to find solutions to make our lives better. We want answers and we want them now!

In general, we focus on **getting the right answer not on asking the right questions.** Why is this? Perhaps it stems from an innate curiosity and a desire to make sense of the world. Perhaps it comes from a fear of the unknown or the need for a quick fix. It may also result from the need for blind acceptance of some *truth* where any form of questioning is strongly discouraged or denied. Perhaps we think we already have the answer, so why ask any questions at all? Whatever the case, there is no doubt human beings like answers.

When we focus on "getting the right answers," rather than "asking the right questions," we limit ourselves. We move into dualistic thinking: "I either have the right answer or I don't." We think in terms of yes or no, right or wrong, good or bad. **This black and white framework enables only surface inquiry**, at best, and quells deeper investigation and the ability to engage with others in meaningful ways. We lose the opportunity to generate new solutions to old problems.

Why are asking the right questions important? Because they generate beneficial lasting change. Empowering questions make possible diverse perspectives, which in turn lead to sustainable solutions to complicated challenges. They enable people to engage in dynamic transformational conversations out of which new ideas are born.

To generate the type of change our world needs, **we must raise penetrative questions to challenge current assumptions**; assumptions that keep us disempowered to affect change. The key in creating a positive, empowering future is asking positive, empowering questions now! So, what are you waiting for?

About the Authors

Kathy Jo Slusher, PCC, ELI-MP, Founder of Marketing Tao, LLC, has dedicated her life to help service-based socially conscious business owners make their business a success through sharing their passion. She believes that when your intention is on your passion and helping others, money is a natural bi-product. *It's not what you sell but what you stand for that makes you a success.* She is deeply committed to helping soloprofessionals and small business owners implement mindful marketing techniques and strategies to attract their ideal clients while making a difference in the world.

Kathy Jo is a Co-Founder of The REAL Results Coaching Exchange, partner in Coaching Skills for Leaders, a member of the International Coach Federation, and Vice-President of the United Nations Association of the US, Indianapolis Chapter.

Denny Balish, PCC, ELI-MP, Professional Certified Coach and Founder of ThreeFold Life Coaching, has dedicated her life's work to the development of Human Potential. She believes that each person has within themselves the desire and ability to be a positive force for change in the world and, by sharing one's unique gifts and talents with others, global change is possible. Denny is deeply committed to helping people and organizations get and stay powerfully on-purpose so they can be the change they wish to see in the world. Denny is a member of the International Coach Federation (ICF), Association for Global New Thought (AGNT), and founding board member of Spirit's Light Foundation, an alternative youth and family ministry with the Association of Unity Churches International.

Other Valuable Resources

For Coaches, Consultants, and Service-Based Small Businesses

 **Ultimate Questions Books**

The real power in transformation is not in the answers, but in the questions we ask. If coaches, therapists or consultants are unsure of the questions to ask, client results are greatly impacted.

This series of books is specifically designed for coaches, consultants, therapists and others who are in a place where they need some fresh ideas to get themselves, a client, or anyone else unstuck. www.UltimateQuestionsBook.com

 **Marketing Made Practical**

Marketing Made Practical is a Home Study Program designed for those who are overwhelmed with all the options and don't have a handle on how to make the marketing process into an effective, successful strategy.

Marketing Made Practical is specifically designed for service-based soloprofessionals or small business owners who are just getting started or have a limited experience and need an organized approach to marketing. www.MarketingMadePractical.com

 **Marketing Strategies University**

Marketing Strategies University is an online training program that walks you through how to create a strong marketing and business development plan.

Marketing Strategies University cuts to the chase of marketing. We don't dive into the theory of marketing – but focus on practical steps to create and implement powerful marketing strategies.

This unique online training program is designed for service-based soloprofessionals or small business owners who have reached a certain level in their business where they are ready to create the systems and strategies for their marketing to take them to the next level of success. www.MarketingStrategiesUniversity.com

 **Marketing Strategies Success**

Marketing Strategies Success is an online membership forum which brings together motivation and information into a community of like-minded business owners all working to create change through their business.

Through topic specific open Q & A calls & recordings, to an interactive forum where members share ideas, to a mentoring component of Success Stories, where successful entrepreneurs share their success secrets, this group will help those who have a message to share through their business but need marketing know-how & structure to accomplish their mission. www.MarketingStrategiesSuccess.com

For Leadership Development Support

 **Coaching Skills for Leaders**

Employees don't leave companies, they leave managers.

According to the Gallup Poll, 71% of employees studied said they were either not engaged or actively disengaged at work. This employee disengagement results in $370 Billion lost annually. That's a huge amount.

In today's environment, talented individuals are arguably an organization's most valuable resource. Yet studies show, high potential employees have a higher turnover rate than any other employee population.

Leaders need to be flexible, adaptable, creative and resourceful to deal with the reality of our economic times. Coaching Skills for Leaders will take you and your organization through The Coaching Clinic, a specialized training program where you acquire a new approach to old issues. This

process offers a step-by-step process of a coaching conversation in how to conduct & lead those difficult conversations. You will learn how to address organizational challenges through a step-by-step structured approach to facilitate your own coaching conversation, and develop partners and accountability standards across the board. Thus you will be transforming managers into true Leaders. www.Coaching-Skills-for-Leaders.com

 Lifestyle, Leadership, Legacy

What are you working for?

As a business owner or executive you've worked hard to get where you are at. But how has this helped the lifestyle you want to lead? If you're tired to living to work instead of working to live, this program is for you.

We will identify your desired lifestyle, look at how to improve your leadership ability so you can more effectively lead those around you as well as your own life and create a lasting legacy to leave behind.

 On-Purpose Leadership Development

For on-purpose professionals who want to develop their leadership acumen while expanding their consciousness. This program formulates a plan of action to break through all obstacles limiting your success, while building powerful skills to help you lead with purpose, including: manage conflict and chaos with greater ease, use your intuition for effortless decision-making, communicate effectively and persuasively, maximize your ability to engage and influence people in positive ways, and feel empowered to affect change in yourself and others.

For Specialized Support for Non-Profits, Social Enterprises and Cultural Creatives

 ### Life Purpose Coaching

Empowering individuals in their midlife years to create a life of deeper meaning and purpose by not only connecting with their authentic voice and innate wisdom, but also by helping them aligning their skills, talents and interests with their desire to give back in meaningful ways.

 ### On-Purpose Career Transition

For individuals in all phases of career and job transition who seek to purposefully align their skills and abilities with their passion for a satisfying career; one that enables them to give back in meaningful ways. Make a living while making a difference! This program is customized to fit individual needs.

For More Information Contact:

Marketing Tao, LLC   **Threefold Life**

Kathy Jo Slusher   Denny Balish

Email   info@MarketingTao.com   Email   info@threefoldlife.com
Call   317.536.5544   Call   708.209.6977
Click   www.MarketingTao.com   Click   www.Threefoldlife.com
Click   www.TheREALResultsCoachingExchange.com